LIFE UNWRAPPED
WORKBOOK

_____

NAME

INTRODUCTION
The Super Silly One
What Superpowers do Christians have?

In other words, what can you do now that you couldn't before? What if I told you there is a spiritual Kryptonite that can disable your new powers either partially or totally? An element of this earth, so strong, that it can render the Holy Spirit powerless in your life. This substance, which is mined in the lowest depths of Hades, is the most valuable currency in the Kingdom of Darkness.

However, unlike Kryptonite, this vile ore must be ingested or in some way inserted into the heart of a super Christian to affect them. This horrid mineral substance is called **Injurite Offensepyrite.** The longer this evil venom stays lodged in the heart, the more it is deposited into the spirit body's bloodstream and soon infection sets in causing a wide variety of symptoms. Symptoms of **"Resentanoid Shame-aphrenia"** may begin with loss of joy and peace and then graduate to marked doubtfulness, and insecurity, and eventually lead to anger, resentment, self-pity, isolation and spiritual amnesia. The condition can be fatal.

ONE FURTHER NOTE.
Avoidance of enemy injections is futile. Only one has ever remained completely immune. That's why God killed him to use his blood to create the anti-serum.

To counter the effects of Injurite Offensepyrite, the antiserum **"Agape"** as it is called, will not only reverse the symptoms and eliminate infection but will completely rid the spirit body of all trace elements of Injurite Offensepyrite.
Because the tactics of the enemy are so relentless and seductive, it is recommended that all Super Christians take a daily dose of Agape. Only a continual supplement of Agape can guarantee the Super Christian against infection. Advanced Resentanoid Shame-aphrenia will cause severe paranoia causing the Super Christian to imagine other Super Christians are enemy agents. Isolation ensues and, in some cases Super Christians have even been known to injure and kill one another under this delusion.

SO, KEEP YOUR GUARD UP, TAKE YOUR AGAPE SUPPLEMENT DAILY!

THIS MESSAGE IS BROUGHT TO YOU BY:
DR. GABRIEL ANGELOS, P.H.D. S.M.D.
SURGEON GENERAL of THE UNIVERSE.

INTRODUCTION

The Super Serious One

Unresolved shame is the most debilitating spiritual condition with which we contend today. **It is the root of almost all Christian inconsistency.**

There Are Three Fundamental Relationships In Life.

> They are:
> 1. My Relationship with _____
>
> 2. My Relationship with _____
>
> 3. My Relationship with _____

The relationships are specified in **Mark 12:29-31;** *29 And Jesus answered him, The first of all the commandments is, Hear O Israel; The Lord our God is one Lord: 30 And thou shalt love the Lord thy God with all thy heart, and with all thy soul, and with all thy mind, and with all thy strength: this is the first commandment. 31 And the second is like, namely this, Thou shalt **love thy neighbor as thyself.** There is none other commandment greater than these.*

The opposite condition of love in these three relationships is Unlove caused by **Unforgiveness.** This unlove/unforgiveness manifests differently in each relationship.

> 1. In My Relationship with God, it is _____
>
> 2. In My Relationship with Others, it is _____
>
> 3. In My Relationship with Myself, it is _____

Unfortunately, many Christians don't feel saved!

4

I WANT TO FEEL SAVED! What keeps us from feeling saved?

The answer is **UNFORGIVENESS** or **UNLOVE**. What if I told you there was a secret passage to **HAPPINESS?**
The secret passage to Christian Happiness is simply **LOVE**. SIMPLE, BUT NOT EASY. But the way to love is the removal of unlove!
To become unconscious of the events that caused unforgiveness.

We can rest when we harbor no offenses.
WE FEEL SAVED when we have no offense *(Shame)* against ourselves!

Session 1:
THE FORGIVENESS FACTOR

Matt 18:21-35; 21 Then Peter came up and said to him, "Lord, how often will my brother sin against me, and I forgive him? **As many as seven times?**" **22** Jesus said to him, "I do not say to you seven times, **but seventy-seven times.**

23 "Therefore the kingdom of heaven may be compared to a king who wished to settle accounts with his servants. **24** When he began to settle, one was brought to him who owed him **ten thousand talents. 25** And since he could not pay, his master ordered him to be sold, with his wife and children and all that he had, and payment to be made. **26** So the servant fell on his knees, imploring him, 'Have patience with me, and I will pay you everything.' **27** And out of pity for him, the master of that servant **released him and forgave him the debt.**

28 But when that same servant went out, he found one of his fellow servants who owed him **a hundred denarii,** and seizing him, he began to choke him, saying, 'Pay what you owe.' **29** So his fellow servant fell down and pleaded with him, 'Have patience with me, and I will pay you.' **30 He refused** and went and put him in prison until he should pay the debt.

31 When his fellow servants saw what had taken place, they were greatly distressed, and they went and reported to their master all that had taken place. **32** Then his master summoned him and said to him, 'You wicked servant! **I forgave you all that debt** because you pleaded with me. **33** And should not you have had mercy on your fellow servant, as I had mercy on you?'

34 And in anger his master **delivered him to the jailers**, until he should pay **all his debt.**

35 So also my heavenly Father will do to every one of you, if you do not forgive your brother from your heart."

1. THE EFFECTS OF UNFORGIVENESS

Un-forgiveness is the most damaging of all sins because:

A. It seems evident that unforgiveness removes the blood from previously forgiven sins, opening the door for me to struggle with all of my old habits, desires, etc.

> **Matt:32** ...*I forgave you all that debt...*

> **Matt 18:34;** *In anger his master turned him over the jailers to be tortured, until he should pay back all he owed.* **(NIV)**

The man had already been forgiven of this debt, but his unforgiveness made him liable for it again. This "debt" was his past sins.

Unforgiveness is the only sin that can provoke God to remove the Blood from previously forgiven sin.

> **Psalm 90:8 ESV;** *You have set our iniquities before you, our secret sins in the light of your presence.*

> **When You Say, "I Can't Forgive."**
> **You Are Saying, "I Can't Be Saved!"**

B. Un-Forgiveness Prevents God From Answering My Prayers, Especially The Prayer Of Repentance.

Mark 11:24-25; *24 Therefore I tell you, whatever you ask in prayer, believe that you have received it, and it will be yours. 25 And whenever you stand praying, forgive, if you have anything against anyone, so that your Father also who is in heaven may forgive you your trespasses. **(ESV)***

C. Un-Forgiveness Turns My Life Over The "The Tormentors."

Matt 18:34-35; *34 And in anger his master delivered him to the jailers, until he should pay all his debt. 35 So also my heavenly Father will do to every one of you, if you do not forgive your brother from your heart."* **(ESV)**

1. Many Christians have NO joy, peace, contentment, direction, purpose, etc. in their walk with God.

2. They don't have a clue as to why their lives are like this either. In their minds, they are doing everything that they know to do and nothing is going right for them.

THEY ARE LIVING IN TORMENT!

Why are they tormented? They have excused the presence of unforgiveness in their hearts.
Nothing will ever change for them until they **"forgive every one his brother their trespasses."**

We must decide, I'd rather be right with God, than right in this disagreement.

D. Unforgiveness Places Me In Spiritual Bondage (Prison)

Matthew 5:21-26; *"You have heard that it was said to those of old, 'You shall not murder; and whoever murders will be liable to judgment.'*

But I say to you that everyone who is angry with his brother will be liable to judgment; whoever insults his brother will be liable to the council; and whoever says, 'You fool!' will be liable to the hell of fire.

So if you are offering your gift at the altar and there **remember that your brother has something against you**, *leave your gift there before the altar and go. First be reconciled to your brother, and then come and offer your gift.*

Come to terms quickly with your accuser while you are going with him to court, lest your accuser hand you over to the judge, and the judge to the guard, **and you be put in prison.**

Truly, I say to you, you will never get out until you have paid the last penny. **(ESV)**

When you don't agree with YOUR adversary, then, "THE" adversary (the devil) puts you in his prison!

E. Unforgiveness Gives Satan An Advantage Over Us.

2 Corinthians 2:10-11; 10 To whom ye forgive any thing, I forgive also: for if I forgave any thing, to whom I forgave it, for your sakes forgave I it in the person of Christ; **11** Lest Satan should get an advantage of us: for we are not ignorant of his devices**. (KJV)**

You can't forgive everybody on your own. You need God's help to forgive them.

Unforgiveness renders us helpless to defend ourselves against the Devil. This inability to defend ourselves will continue to intensify until we are completely under his influence.

2. THE REALIZATION OF UNFORGIVENESS

A. How Do You Know If You Have Un-Forgiveness In Your Heart?
We tend to overlook unforgiveness in our hearts. Forgiveness isn't just words it's a change of heart towards the offender

(Old arguments are indicative of un-forgiveness.)
The rule of thumb is; **If you can feel it, He ain't healed it!**
In other words, if pondering a situation or a person provokes negative feelings, this is evidence enough of un-forgiveness.

If an encounter with an individual causes you discomfort or gives rise to such feelings as, resentment, anger, fear, disgust, etc. then it is a given that you have an issue of un-forgiveness against them or someone connected to them.
If you will simply begin to pray blessings on everyone in your life you will soon discover hidden unforgiveness.

(Be careful, some prayers may get stuck in your throat).

In a later section, we will discuss in detail the actual mechanics of agape forgiveness. But for now, we will use the simple tool of prayer.

Let's pause from our notes for 5 minutes and begin the assignment on the next page and then we will return to the lesson. *Some of the hardest names to write down are good people that you also love because it's possible to love and hate the same person.*

TO BE FORGIVEN
(If you get stuck, just scroll through your contact list)

3. THE POWER OF FORGIVENESS

A. Only God Has The Power To Forgive

Let's read Mark 2:1-12; *And when he returned to Capernaum after some days, it was reported that he was at home. 2 And many were gathered together, so that there was no more room, not even at the door. And he was preaching the word to them. 3 And they came, bringing to him a paralytic carried by four men. 4 And when they could not get near him because of the crowd, they removed the roof above him, and when they had made an opening, they let down the bed on which the paralytic lay. 5 And when Jesus saw their faith, he said to the paralytic, "Son, your sins are forgiven."*

6 Now some of the scribes were sitting there, questioning in their hearts, 7 "Why does this man speak like that? He is blaspheming! Who can forgive sins but God alone?" 8 And immediately Jesus, perceiving in his spirit that they thus questioned within themselves, said to them, "Why do you question these things in your hearts? 9 Which is easier, to say to the paralytic, 'Your sins are forgiven,' or to say, 'Rise, take up your bed and walk'? 10 But that you may know that the Son of Man has authority on earth to forgive sins"—he said to the paralytic— 11"I say to you, rise, pick up your bed, and go home." 12 And he rose and immediately picked up his bed and went out before them all, so that they were all amazed and glorified God, saying, "We never saw anything like this!"

It is humanly impossible to forgive!
It is also humanly impossible to cast out devils, heal the sick, discern spirits, prophecy & many other Biblical directives! Yet we are told to do all these things.

Only God has the power to cast out devils, heal the sick, discern spirits, prophecy, etc. **Only God has the power to forgive.**

Through His enabling grace, so can we!
Therefore, FORGIVENESS becomes a miracle done through FAITH!
  B. Forgive Through Christ.

  2 Corinthians 2:10-11; 10 *To whom ye forgive any thing, I forgive also: for if I forgave any thing, to whom I forgave it, for your sakes forgave I it in the person of Christ;* **11** *Lest Satan should get an advantage of us: for we are not ignorant of his devices.* **(KJV)**

4. The Process of Forgiveness

  A. Pray For Your Enemies

Jesus said to pray for those who hurt you. This is the process by which His grace can heal us.

As we pray for those on our Forgiveness list, we will begin to experience breakthroughs that will lead to emotional healing and deliverance from torments. One reason that your gospel experience hasn't netted the spiritual power that it should over weakness and sin is because of unforgiveness.

  B. Jesus Gave Us The "200%" Principle.

Matthew 5 verses 21-22 Teaches us to deal with **my offense** against my brother.
Verses 23-26 Teaches us how to deal with a brother who is offended with us. **(Others who are offended)**
We are not instructed here to go to a brother when we are offended, as we have always been taught. This can create even more offense.

We should go to a brother to help him to forgive us!

C. Forgiving God?

Acts 24:16; *So I always take pains to have a clear conscience toward both God and man.*

1. Paul confessed to having a history of offense towards God. It is both normal and biblical to struggle with offense against God.

2. Perceived offense is just as real as actual offense.
If you believe that God has failed you, rejected you, or not loved you enough to protect you from various tragedies in your life then it is just as painful and effective as if he had failed, rejected, or ignored your plight.

3. Forgiving God? What the heck is that?
Forgiving God is simply repenting of the lies that you have believed about Him.

Put these offenses against God on your prayer list. Talk to Him about it. Ask Him to forgive you for believing a lie about Him. Renounce the lie. Replace the lie with a truth.

4. Don't let Satan interpret the drama of your life.
Consider the possibility that if those painful happenings had not been included in the recipe of your life you may not be serving the Lord today or you may not be as useful in His kingdom as you are today or will be someday.

Sometimes it is the very trauma and tragedy that made us open and willing to hear the Gospel and receive salvation. There is something to be said for the pain of my past driving me to the cross. It served a purpose, but now that purpose is finished. Now, the purpose of my pain is to help others. So, I have to get it out of my heart and into my hands.

Let God's love interpret those so-called tragedies of your life.

C. The Prayer of Forgiveness Should Be a Part of Every Prayer Meeting!

Matthew 11:25; *25 And whenever you stand praying, forgive, if you have anything against anyone, so that your Father also who is in heaven may forgive you your trespasses*

The Lord's Prayer
Matthew 6:12-15; Further Emphasizes This Principle.
> *12 and forgive us our sins, as we have forgiven those who sin against us. 13 And don't let us yield to temptation, but rescue us from the evil one. 14 "If you forgive those who sin against you, your heavenly Father will forgive you. 15 But if you refuse to forgive others, your Father will not forgive your sins.*

Some good prayers are…
> Lord, I forgive, help my unforgiveness.
> Lord, I can't but You can through me.
> If you can deliver me from everything else, you can deliver me from un-forgiveness.
> Jesus, I want to walk in the Spirit, but I'm paralyzed by this bitterness! HEAL ME! ***RELEASE IT TO HIM BY FAITH!***

REVIEW: THE FORGIVENESS FACTOR

_____ cannot forgive the unforgiving.

_____ removes the blood from our past sins, opening the door for me to struggle with all my old habits and desires.

Unforgiveness prevents God from answering

my_____.

Unforgiveness turns my life over to the

_____.

Unforgiveness gives Satan an _____ over me.

Unforgiveness puts me in a _____ _____.

_____ is the device of Satan (he is the accuser of the brethren). 2 Corinthians 2:11

When you say I can't forgive'
you are saying I can't ____ _____.

If I can still_____it, God hasn't healed it.

It is both common and_____to struggle with offense against _____. Acts 24:16

It is_____impossible to forgive, it takes a divine work of grace, and this miracle is released by _____.

Session 2: ARE YOU ASHAMED & DON'T KNOW IT?

Remember we started out by saying, **"Unresolved shame is the most debilitating spiritual condition with which we contend today. It is the root of almost all-Christian inconsistency.**

What are the three fundamental relationships in life?

> My relationship with
> 1. _____ 2. _____ 3. _____
>
> *..."And thou shalt love the Lord thy God with all thy heart... and thou shalt love thy neighbor as thyself."*

There is no other commandment greater than these!

The Greek Word for **"love"** in the first two relationships is **"agape,"** therefore the implied word for loving myself must also be "agape."

"Agape" love has its source in God alone. It is not possible for us to produce a love that satisfies God's criteria of what constitutes
"agape love" through our own strength or human emotions.

Therefore, we must do these three things,

1. We must allow God to enable us to love Him.

2. We must allow God to love others through us.

3. It is vitally important that we allow God to love us and to help us love ourselves.

This weekend is about learning to walk in the supernatural love of God. living in the love of God is a miracle.

The **pivotal relationship** of the three is **the way I feel about myself.** Whether or not I am able to love myself affects my ability to love God and others.

If I believe that I am unlovable, I will refuse to allow God to love me.
If I believe that I am not worthy of His love, I will reject His love.
Therefore, I became unloved. He cannot love me against my will.

1. SHAME
Shame is a grudge that I harbor against myself.

Unforgiveness against God manifests itself as rebellion. When you have unforgiveness against others, that's bitterness. Unforgiveness against yourself is **SHAME**. We tend to focus on our victimhood but there are an equal number of perpetrators. For everybody you hate and can't forgive, some people hate and can't forgive you.

That's the shame component of our lives and it's not enough to focus on forgiving others if we don't spend time and focus on forgiving ourselves. One reason some people have a very hard time forgiving someone else is that they won't accept personal responsibility in the event.

You have to get to a point where you can say "I was part of it", "I did things I shouldn't have done", "I said things I shouldn't have said," "I'm gonna forgive me and I'm gonna forgive them". Forgive yourself for what you have done to others and yourself. That's the objective for tonight. This requires an admission, whether it's to someone directly or to yourself.

SHAME DEFINED; Shame is defined as **"the painful feeling of the loss of self-respect."**

A. Shame emphasizes the humiliation felt at the loss of esteem.

    1. Shame includes the idea of feeling humiliated or embarrassed from a sense of inadequacy or inferiority.

    2. Shame also includes the pain caused by losing the respect of others.

B. Shame can only develop through problems in interpersonal relationships that are significant to us.

    1. Shame is always a product of the failure or perceived failure to meet the expectations of someone from whom we desire to receive approval.

    2. This failure results in rejection or perceived rejection.

    3. Therefore, failure and rejection are the key elements of shame.

    4. Suffering rejection from someone I desire to please may result in me rejecting myself.

When I feel that I am not good enough to be accepted by the people that I consider most important to me, I will usually reject myself.

THIS SELF-REJECTION IS CALLED "SHAME"!

C. Shame says to us:

    1. You are a mistake.

    2. You are flawed and defective as a human being.

    3. You will never be good enough.

    4. Everyone will ultimately reject you as soon as they find out what you really are.

    5. You are a failure.

Very often, this self-rejection is connected to a person in our first few years of life, our first 7 years of life, or maybe older. Typically shame is made more powerful in our lives with the human assistance of someone we needed to love and respect us, who instead shamed us and told us lies about ourselves.

2. SOURCES OF SHAME:

A. MY OWN **PAST** ACTIONS & OMMISSIONS

The most obvious sources of shame are:
-   Those things that I did that I wish I had not done
-   Those things that I did not do that I wish I had done. i.e. – sins that I committed that were particularly damaging to me or someone else that I cannot get over or forget about and never feel forgiven for, especially sexual sins (fornication, adultery, homosexuality, etc.)
-   Goals that I did not reach which greatly disappointed me or let someone else down causing me to feel that my life will be forever incomplete.
-   Things that I earnestly intended or greatly desired to do but missed the opportunity to do because of neglect, procrastination, etc. (i.e. –speaking to someone who died before I could get to them, applying for a job, going to college, marrying a certain person, etc.)

WOULDA   COULDA   SHOULDA . . .

What did Paul say could not separate us from the **LOVE** of God?

> **Romans 8:35-39** Who shall separate us from the love of Christ? shall tribulation, or distress, or persecution, or famine, or nakedness, or peril, or sword?...37 Nay, in all these things we are more than conquerors through him that loved us.
> 38 For I am persuaded, that neither death, nor life, nor angels, nor principalities, nor powers, **nor things present, nor things to come,** 39 Nor height, nor depth, nor any other creature, *shall be able to separate us from the love of God*, which is in Christ Jesus our Lord.

Things Present and **Things to Come, he didn't PAST!**
Only things **PAST** can separate you from God's
Love!!!!

3. OTHER KEY SOURCES OF SHAME ARE:

     A. Past Rejection
The real or perceived rejection by someone of significance
to me. i.e. – Withholding of affection

Mental or emotional abuse, usually by means of verbal
abuse *("Why are you so stupid? "You will never amount to
anything. "Why can't you be like your brother?")*

Subconsciously, the rejected person blames themself for
not being able to be good enough or to do good enough to
be accepted.

     B. Past Alienation
This includes the idea of the extremity of alienation, which
is **ABANDONMENT**. ***"Abandon" - forsake; desert***;
Implies leaving a person or thing, either as a final
necessary measure or as a complete rejection of
another's claims, responsibilities, etc.
- Victims of the sexual infidelity of their mate
- Victims of divorce, either the mate or the child
- Victims of a loved one who deserts the family
- Survivors of a loved one who commits suicide

     C. Past Abuse
These are defined as violations of the "person."
- Physical abuse (by parents, spouse, etc.)
- Sexual abuse (statistically, in most cases, the
  perpetrator is a close friend or relative)
- Rape
- Pornography, including being forced to watch the
  indiscriminate sex acts of others. These things
  transfer the feeling of uncleanness to the observer
  as if they had participated in the act themselves.

The perverseness and irony of all types of sins against the person are that the victim subconsciously blames themselves and not the perpetrator, (i.e. - "if I was not such a bad person, they would not be treating me like this")

D. Class Rejection
Shame experienced by a group of people because of rejection experienced as a group.
i.e. - usually the result of persecution, enslavement, defeat in war, being cast out of a larger group, being misunderstood, and being accused of being something that you are not (Jews, Blacks, Christians, etc.)

E. Self-Destructive Behavior
Shame begets more shame. Drug & alcohol abuse, violence, domestic violence, gambling addiction, pornography addiction, food addiction, bulimia, anorexia, self-harm, etc. Shame is the root cause of ALL self-destructive behavior.

4. The Cycle of Shame

A. Shame-Based Identity; *I begin to associate myself with the person that rejection has convinced me that I am - someone worthy of more and more rejection. I become convinced that I am hopelessly flawed as a person and that there is no power within me to change me.*

B. Distorted Thinking; *I become convinced that I need someone or something more than I have within me to be happy, to feel complete, or to feel better about myself. If I could just find something from outside of me that is better than what I have within me, I could become a better person and feel better about myself. This can cause us to search for fulfillment in relationships careers or substance abuse.*

C. Acting Out Feelings; *I resort to searching for ways to fulfill my lust for things, pleasure, etc. This includes drugs, alcohol, adultery, perversion, gluttony, etc.*

D. Life Damaging Consequences; *The results of my actions serve only to severely compound my problems. Now I must deal with the consequences of my actions, which have caused an intensification of my shame beyond my imagination.*

5. THE LIFESTYLE OF SHAME

Shame has a distinctive lifestyle, which is characterized by some specific attitudes, which are especially damaging to ourselves and our interpersonal relationships.

Shame promotes a lifestyle of extremes in which we alternate between the extremes depending on whether we are "up" or "down".

These extremes seem to be contradictory because they are so opposite in their character, but they are identical in nature.

They are simply two sides of the same coin. We manifest a particular extreme depending on whether we are:

> **"Up"** (attempting to hide our flaws, faults, and shame to avoid rejection)

> **"Down"** (unsuccessful in our attempts to hide our shame, we surrender to it. We presume rejection and act in such a way as to produce it)

They are as follows:

A. SUPERIORITY
We attempt to be better than everyone in order to try and convince ourselves we are at least as good

as they are. Superiority is the "smoke screen" behind which we operate.
- Shame will cause you to beat down your spouse and children.
- Shame will cause you to be controlling, manipulative, and self-pitying.

INFERIORITY
We feel beneath everyone, and there is no motivation to attempt to improve ourselves because all such "attempts" would only result in failure. We allow no one the opportunity to reject us because we have already rejected ourselves to such a degree that there is no capacity within us to experience further rejection.

Self-deprecation is a Sin! *(I'm so stupid, I hate myself, I'm a failure, I'm such a jerk, why can't I ever do anything right)*

1 Corinthians 3: 9 & 16 (paraphrased) *9 For we are God's fellow workers. You are God's field, God's building. 16 Do you not know that you are God's temple and that God's Spirit dwells in you?*

*There are **two more** pages of examples, and you are going to spend **5 minutes** reading over them to find yourself in these lifestyles of shame.*

B. CONTROL
We must be in control of all interactions, feelings, and personal behavior at all times. Control is our foremost defense strategy for shame.

PASSIVITY
We let everyone "walk" on us. We stand up for nothing, etc. We fear to voice an opinion or disagree. Doing something that would attract attention to oneself is a terrorizing thought.

C. PERFECTIONISM

We must always be right in everything we do. This involves a measurement that is always being imposed upon self and others. The feat and the avoidance of the negative is the organizing principle of life. Everyone must live up to an externalized image. Of course, no one ever measures up.

DEFEATISM

We are convinced that we can never do anything right, so why try?

D. BLAME

Blame is another defensive cover-up for shame. When things don't turn out as desired, someone else must always be at fault.

SELF-BLAME

Regardless of what has gone wrong, it must be our fault somehow. We see ourselves as the ones at fault for everything!

E. DENIAL OF THE FIVE FREEDOMS

Full functionality as a person is dependent upon the power to perceive, think, and interpret, to feel, to want and choose, and to imagine.

A shame-based lifestyle refuses to allow these freedoms to operate in others freely, fearing that they might come to conclusions different than ours which we would consider as rejection.

DENY OURSELVES THE USE OF THE FIVE FREEDOMS

We refuse to think or objectively consider the facts, lest we come to conclusions different from everyone else's. This would produce an inner conflict over having to stand for what we believe and possibly be rejected or to deny our own conclusions and further erode what remaining self-respect that we may have.

F. NO-TALK RULE
Shame prevents a person from talking about their problems, needs, wants, etc. All true feelings must be kept secret to prevent rejection or embarrassment.

COMPULSION TO INDISCRIMINATELY "TELL ALL"
We feel that we must tell everything we know or think about ourselves to be "honest" with people when all we are attempting to do is to produce the rejection that we have predetermined is going to happen anyway.

G. FEAR OF MISTAKES
Mistakes reveal the flawed vulnerable self. To acknowledge a mistake is to open ourselves to scrutiny. Therefore, we must cover up our own mistakes. If someone else makes a mistake, we must shame them!

ADDICTED TO MAKING MISTAKES
Subconsciously, we become so convinced that we can do nothing right that we produce mistakes as a self-fulfilling prophecy.

H. DISTRUST/SUSPICION
Shame says that one must never expect reliability in relationships. Never trust anyone and you will never be disappointed. The result is that we attempt to go through life trusting no one, but ourselves.

DISTRUST OF SELF
Distrust of self can become one of the most negative emotional conditions with which a person tries to live. It is possible that the result of this attitude could cause a total paralysis of life. We

become so afraid of failing that we cannot bring ourselves to try anything, especially anything new.

6. THE EMOTIONS OF SHAME

Shame has many distinctive emotions. **They are not all human emotions. They are interjected into the human experience as a result of shame.**

Man was not created with these emotions! They are a result of the Sin Nature. When we are saved, we receive the power to reverse the curse and return to our original created state. While this is complete and fully realized Spiritually with God, we must bring the soul into alignment. We do that through the power of forgiveness, the removal of shame, renouncing every lie we believe and embracing opposite truths.

When these emotions exist in an individual, it is proof that shame exists in their being.

Many of these emotions are:
- INFERIORITY
- DEPRESSION
- EMBARRASSMENT or the EXTREME FEAR OF EMBARRASSMENT
- HUMILIATION
- HOPELESSNESS
- LONELINESS
- HELPLESSNESS
- INCOMPLETENESS, feeling of being FLAWED
- DISAPPOINTMENT
- REGRET usually with DEEP SORROW, which can find no relief
- ALIENATION or ABANDONMENT
- UNCLEAN, DIRTY, SOILED
- ABIDING ANGER with a QUICK TEMPER
- UNEXPLAINABLE FEAR or TERROR
- FEAR OF FAILURE, FEAR OF REJECTION

The effect of these emotions is further compounded by visiting spirits of a like nature to these shame-based emotions. In other words, what you are most susceptible to is where evil spirits will attack.

7. SOLUTIONS TO SHAME:
The solution to shame is two-fold.

> **A.** Recognize my intrinsic value as a person created by God. (Self-worth / Self-esteem)

Romans 8:31-32; *What then shall we say to these things? If God is for us, who can be against us? He who did not spare his own Son but gave him up for us all, how will he not also with him graciously give us all things?* **(ESV)**

1 John 3:16; *By this we know love, that he laid down his life for us.* **(ESV)**

I must be worth a tremendous amount to Him because He died for me and is for me!

I Had This Value As A Sinner, Even Before He Further Invested In Me! Because Of My Created Worth!

John 3:16; *For God so **loved the world,** that he gave his only begotten Son, that whosoever believeth in him should not perish, but have everlasting life.*

Ephesians 2:4-6; *But God, who is rich in mercy, **for his great love wherewith he loved us,** 5 Even when we were dead in sins, hath quickened us together with Christ, (by grace ye are saved;) 6 And hath raised us up together, and made us sit together in heavenly places in Christ Jesus…*

Romans 5:5-8; *5 and hope does not put us to shame, because God's love has been poured into our hearts through the Holy Spirit who has been given to us. 6 For while we were still weak, at the right time **Christ died for the ungodly.** 7 For one will scarcely die for a righteous person—though perhaps for a good person one would dare even to die—8 but God shows his love for us in that **while we were still sinners,** Christ died for us.*

You had so much worth, even in your worst condition. In your worst state, as your worst self, you had created worth. The devil hated you before you became a Christian because you were created in the image of God.

You are the only creation that looks like Jesus Christ. You have mannerisms and personality traits that resemble God. In your worst condition, you're loved by God enough for Him to send His Son to Calvary.

You have to recognize that you've done nothing to earn that agape. You were created by God to be loved by Him. He loves everyone on the planet equally.

       B. Believe and accept God's Love for me.

1 John 3:1; *See **what kind of love the Father has given to us,** that we should be called children of God; and so we are. The reason why the world does not know us is that it did not know him.*

1. *Accepting His love without reservation is the channel through which I receive everything that God does for me: naturally or spiritually.*

You haven't received more from God because you don't believe He loves you. If God let you earn it, if God answered your prayers and did all kinds of things for you based on your current condition of not really believing that He loves you, it would reinforce your shame. It would reinforce your superiority and all the negative particles of your shame-based identity. You would then believe that you earned it, you were good enough, you achieved it.

The bottom line is God can only trust us with His amazing gifts and blessings when we understand that we've received them because He loves us and for no other reason. When we see someone else being blessed, we also have to understand they're being blessed, not because they're better than us, but because He loves them too.

This changes everything for us. It will raise the ceiling on the supernatural and the miraculous in your life infinitely.

1 John 4:19 & 16; *"We love him, because he first loved us."* **v16** *"And we have **known** and **believed** the love that God hath to us. God is love; and he that dwelleth in love dwelleth in God, and God in him."*

I must exercise my **FAITH**, to believe His **Love** for me!

Hebrews 4:1-2, 9, 11 KJV
1 Let us therefore fear, lest, a promise being left us of entering into his rest, any of you should seem to come short of it. 2 For unto us was the gospel preached, as well as unto them: but the word preached did not profit them, not being mixed with faith in them that heard it...9 There remaineth therefore a rest to the people of God...11 Let us labour therefore to enter into that rest, lest any man fall after the same example of unbelief.

We must believe in the love of God, the goodness of God, the goodness of people, and the redemption of people.

Unbelief equals believing something else.

When we struggle to believe in God's love for us personally, it's because we believe somebody else. We must identify the lies we believe, put them on trial, and expunge them from our lives.

We must recognize that the someone else we're believing is the devil. Therefore, unbelief is believing a lie about God, others, or self.

Every shortcoming, every struggle, every problem, and every pain in your life is inextricably linked to a lie you believe. The only power the devil has over any believer is his lies.

2. If I don't allow God to love me unconditionally, He **cannot** save me, heal me, supply my needs, or answer my prayers.

> **His love is the conduit through which all of His Blessings flow to us.**

3. He will NOT meet my needs for the purpose of enabling me to feel that I have earned something from Him. He ONLY meets our needs to communicate to us how He feels about us.

4. My performance does not produce relationships. Relationship with Him produces performance!

5. He loves us because of **WHO WE ARE** not because of what we do. **SHAME PREVENTS US FROM BELIEVING THIS!**

GOD IS NOT TIRED OF FORGIVING YOU!

There is nothing my daughter or son can do to cause me not to love them. Am I greater than God? God requires me to forgive my neighbor 70 X 7 times per day. Am I greater than God? Does God expect more forgiveness from me than He is willing to give to me?

God is not tired of forgiving you. He does not tire.

GOD LOVES YOU!

Jeremiah 31:3; *the Lord appeared to him from far away.* ***I have loved you with an everlasting love***; *therefore I have continued my* ***faithfulness to you***.

You have Created worth! His fingerprints are on the clay. There is a family resemblance; you were made in His image. The devil hates you because you look like God.

You have Calvary worth! His blood is flowing in our spiritual hearts. His Spirit is in our spirits. His blessings are invested into our lives. No wonder one soul is worth more than the whole world!

> *The solution to shame is simple - let God love you. Believe God loves you. Believe you're worth it all to Him. The battle of shame is fought by focusing on the truth of God's love and shame melts away.*

*WHEN WE GET A REVELATION OF OUR VALUE TO GOD, AND HIS GREAT LOVE FOR US, THEN WE CAN RELEASE OURSELVES OF THE GRUDGES OF SHAME WE ARE HOLDING AGAINST OURSELVES AND FREELY ACCEPT **HIS LOVE!***

We must…
- **Forgive God,** (the grudge of rebellion & doubt)
- **Forgive Others,** (the grudge of bitterness
- **Forgive Ourselves** of the (grudge of shame)

Just set it down at his feet & leave it there!
Accept His love unconditionally.
Let God love you.

Mirror, Mirror On The Wall, Who's The Real Me After All? Do I see the things I've done, the places I've been, the mistakes I've made? Or do I see the one that God loves? Because that's the real me. Not my achievements. Not my failures. My identity is simply *loved by God.* Everything else is inconsequent. I am loved by God. This is my true identity. That's all I need to know about myself. I am the one God loves.

Review –
ARE YOU ASHAMED & DON'T KNOW IT?

God cannot forgive the unforgiving.

Unforgiveness removes the blood from our past sins, opening the door for me to struggle with all my old habits and desires. Matthew 18:21-35
Unforgiveness prevents God from answering my prayers.

Unforgiveness turns my life over to the tormentors.

Unforgiveness gives Satan an advantage over me. II Cor. 2:10

Unforgiveness puts me in a spiritual prison.

Unforgiveness is the device of Satan (he is the accuser of the brethren). II Corinthians. 2:11

If I can still feel it, God hasn't healed it.

It is humanly impossible to forgive, it takes a divine work of grace, and this miracle is released to me by faith. II Cor. 2:10 and Mark 2:1-12

It is both common and Biblical to struggle with offense against God. Acts 24:16

Reconciliation is so important to God that he allows His enemy to _____ and _____ His own children who fail to reconcile and find agreement.

We must continually deal with offenses against God, others, and _____.

It is common to have unforgiveness against self, this is called shame.

_____.love is God's love. It is a supernatural love.

I am _____ to love myself supernaturally; this can only be accomplished through faith.

I must allow _____ to love me. This is accomplished by faith.

Session 3: INTERPRETING THE DRAMA OF YOUR LIFE

Where did my emotional problems begin?
Why did I always feel like an outsider, a reject, even as a small child?
How much of it was genetic?
Why can some people experience social trauma and come out seemingly unscathed, while others take every injury to heart?

There are two main elements at work.

Nature and Nurture.

Nature-Genetics, Nurture-experience, and environment.
In nature and nurture, there are various controls that when established or ignored will limit or exaggerate the effect that all other nurturing will have.

Your negative natures (genes) and positive natures are nurtured by experiences and environment.

As I've said, in nature and nurture there are these controls, which profoundly influence this experiment called life.

In nurture (experience and environment) one profoundly influencing voice can enhance or diminish the effect of all other nurturing (positive and negative).

To narrow this down:
> The most important of these (controls) is the God-instituted role of a father.

If a father is **encouraging and supportive**
- Then the criticisms in a person's life will have less of a sting. Rejections will have less impact. Praise will be heard and believed.

On the other hand, if the father **is critical and unsupportive** the opposite will likely be true.
- Criticism will be heard and believed and impact the psychological development of the child. Praise and encouragement will be suspected of ulterior motives or simply ignored.

No doubt there is a wide continuum in this principle, and we may find ourselves at all different degrees of development based on our varied experiences.

When a father is absent, He will be replaced either intentionally or accidentally, but the void will be filled, and influence, good or bad, will be established.

At an early age, the systematic habit of assimilating experiences and assigning their meaning is fully developed. The meaning assigned determines the impact of the experience.

A 4-year-old experiences trauma and decides what it means. Thirty years later, the 34-year-old still subscribes to the 4-year-old's opinion.

From very early on, the person interprets life through this established filter. Right or wrong, good or bad, the lens through which they view others, themselves, and God, has been crafted.

Few are ever able to reinvent this paradigm.
Those who do, know there are several guiding dynamics that empower their change.

1. The acknowledging of:
>   Their need to change. Their brokenness.
>   The possibility for change.

2. The will to change.
>   To persevere.
>
>   The discipline to continually
>
>   readjust.
>
>   The energy to invest time re-
>
>   educating, re-nurturing & re-
>
>   experiencing life.

3. The Humility to continue to embrace the above-stated.

4. Choosing to believe and embrace a new truth about God, myself, and others.

5. Redefining & interpreting past experience and embedding those definitions into my language, emotions, and logic.

6. Turning our mourning into praise (Isaiah *61)*

7. Forgiving and accepting forgiveness.

The dominant need to be right will seek agreement in your life with your story and ignore or forget everything else. When something or someone does not fit our story, we will unconsciously attempt to force them into a role or behavior that will prove us right.

Interpreting the Drama of Your Life

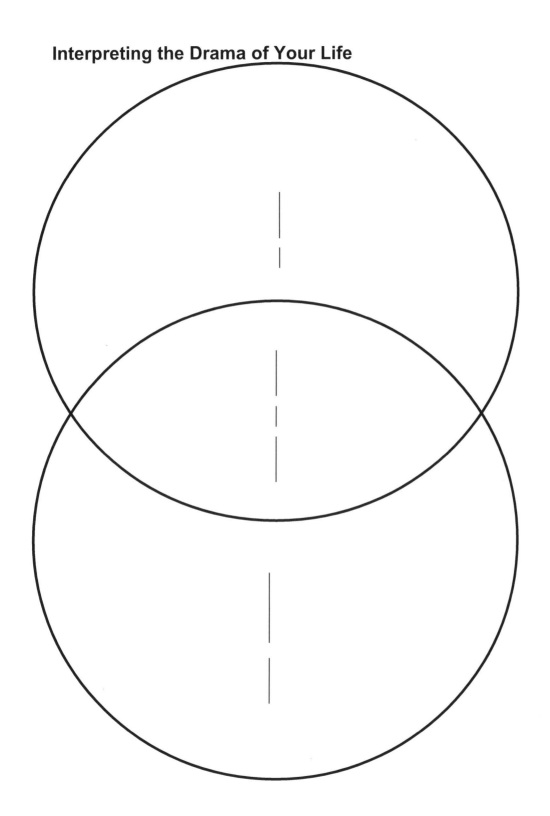

PROPER INTERPRETATION

So, do we interpret the Drama of our lives? Yes, to an extent. Does it play a role in God's Plan for our lives and ministries? Of course.

I even believe some of my drama was retroactive answers to my own prayers for use in His Kingdom.

Was it all for the Glory of God that He could save & use me anyway? Absolutely! Even some of it, if not all of it, was part of the recipe of my salvation. But let's put it in context.

> **Romans 3:23;** *For all have sinned, and come short of the glory of God;*

Original sin is that sin nature that we inherit.
Tragic events abound in the earth and most often in lives not in fellowship with God and which will never fulfill spiritual destiny. Because sin reigns, evil is enthroned in this natural world. Rebellion is the norm.

Before you try to find too much meaning and put everything on God, just understand that everybody on this planet has free will. Most of them use their free will to gratify their own desires regardless of the impact on others. That's the world we live in. Most people live through all of that for no purpose at all and then they die.

You could have drama without faith. Most do.
So, first understand that God didn't force or will tragedy on your life.
It is the natural lay of the landscape of humanity.
There is a destructive spiritual force at work in the world.

Add to this, evil people possessing free will, (the choice or option to do evil) and you have a climate of infectious evil where no one is exempt from injury. Many are the eternal casualties.

We, however, have chosen to respond to the call of grace. God in His foreknowledge knew we would do so, and He predestinated our lives. This simply means, he measured and carefully arranged the types of offenses, the degree of offense, and the administration of spiritual remedies into our lives.

> God's plan does not introduce offense and injury to us, but He can boundary it, define its limits, and give purpose to it.

> What would otherwise be sin and chaos becomes, by His oversight, a ministry prescription.

Where sin and offense would have dominated my life, because of grace, it becomes a servant to my life. My destiny and ultimately accounts for my eternal reward!

What happened doesn't change, **BUT** what it means to you and your story does! Rewrite what happened but with your new meanings and your new story.

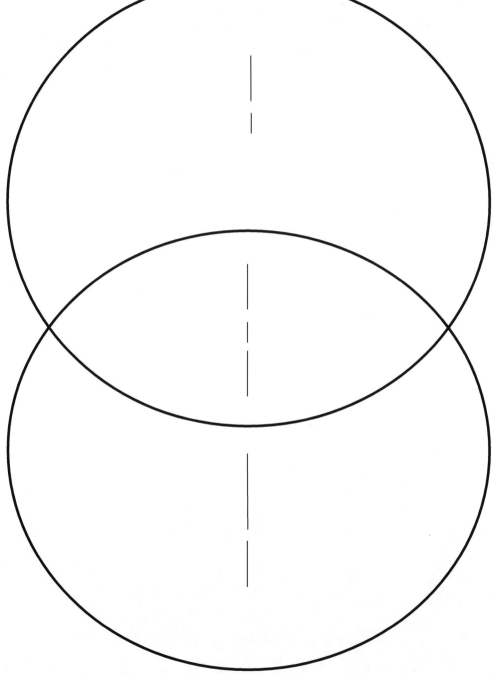

I DECLARE

It doesn't mean what I thought it meant.

It doesn't mean what the devil said it meant.

Some of it may not mean anything.

I will not fully understand it until I reach heaven, but I can be healed and use my experience of pain and healing to help others find their way to God and emotional health.

I will get my past out of my heart and into my hands.

I will use it to work for Him instead of letting it work on me.

I am free from yesterday and I am racing toward the future with enthusiasm.

I am a shame conqueror!

Session 4: TOOL TIME
(THE MECHANICS OF AGAPE FORGIVENESS)

THE WILL OF GOD IS FOR US TO BE WHOLE

> **Luke 4:18;** *The Spirit of the Lord is upon me, because he hath anointed me to preach the gospel to the poor; he hath sent me to heal the brokenhearted, to preach deliverance to the captives, and recovering of sight to the blind, to set at liberty them that are bruised, (KJV)*

This last sentence does not make sense at face value. The definition of the word bruised used here translates to "Life-shattering events."

However, it does make perfect sense when you understand the principle of being spiritually bound, imprisoned and even tortured by the enemy because of unforgiveness. People who have suffered life-shattering trauma end up imprisoned by it emotionally and spiritually and much of their life is a reaction to the past.

Jesus not only came to seek and to save the lost, but he also came to heal and deliver us.

10 TOOLS FOR RECEIVING & MAINTAINING AGAPE LOVE

TOOL #1 Releasing

Releasing Offense & Becoming Immune to Shame

A. There Was Nothing **IN** Jesus That Satan Could Use To Overpower Him!

John 14:30; *I will no longer talk much with you, for the ruler of this world is coming, and he has nothing in Me.*

AMP – "...he has no claim on me - he has nothing in common with me, there is nothing in me that belongs to him, he has no power over me."
PHILLIPS – "...he has no hold on me."
NIV – "...he has no effect on me."
NEB – "...he has no rights over me."

Jesus made it clear why He enjoyed such success against Satan and why He had no fear of Satan or his influence upon Him:

THERE WAS NOTHING IN JESUS THAT SATAN COULD USE TO OVERPOWER HIM!

> **B.** Offense Or Unforgiveness Is The Property Of Satan. Getting You To Hold On To It For Him, Is his Tactic.

If we are to be free from shame, we must identify and deal with those things in our hearts that Satan is claiming as his and that he is using to gain access to our hearts to exercise influence over us.

In other words, unrealized grudges against myself cause shame & serve as an inroad for the enemy into my heart, (which is to say, my logical, emotional & volitional man.)

> **Galatians 5:1;** *"Stand fast therefore in the liberty wherewith Christ has made us free, and be not entangled again with the yoke of bondage."*

TOOL #2 Believing The Truth

Believing the truth has to do with the mind and its renewal.

      A. The Truth is God's Perspective

We Need A Proper Interpretation Of The Past & Present

By redefining the events of our lives through the love of God we can then write a new story about ourselves and begin believing that story about ourselves by faith.

      B. The Real War is in Your Mind

Commonly, when people think "Spiritual Warfare" they only think about the war happening in the Spiritual Realm as seen in Ephesians 6:10-13; *Finally, my brethren, be strong in the Lord, and in the power of his might. **11** Put on the whole armor of God, that ye may be able to stand against the wiles of the devil. **12** For we wrestle not against flesh and blood, but against principalities, against powers, against the rulers of the darkness of this world, against spiritual wickedness in high places. **13** Wherefore take unto you the whole armor of God...*

But The Real War is in Your Mind.

The Greater Spiritual Warfare is personal/mental.
    2 Corinthians 10:3-6; *For though we walk in the flesh, we do not war after the flesh: **4** (For the weapons of our warfare are not carnal, but mighty through God to the **pulling down** of strong holds;)*
    5 Casting down *imaginations, and every high thing that exalteth itself against the knowledge of God, and*

bringing into captivity every thought to the obedience of Christ; 6 And having in a readiness to revenge all disobedience, when your obedience is fulfilled.

Defeating spiritual entities is likened to wrestling. But defeating the carnal mind is like DESTROYING A FORTIFIED CASTLE.

This is why people can be useful in God's kingdom to a degree and never maintain agape healing. They invest most of their energy into corporate battles for ministry victories and not enough into personal battles for personal victory.

C. The Intoxication Of Mental Snares

2 Timothy 2:25-26; *In meekness instructing those that oppose themselves; if God peradventure will give them repentance to the acknowledging of the truth. 26 And that they may RECOVER themselves out of the snare of the devil, who are taken captive by him at his will.*

A person captured must be taught how to extricate themself from the Devil's snare.

RECOVER ananepho (an-an-ay'-fo) to become sober again, i.e. (figuratively) regain (one's) senses:

RECOVER (VINE'S) ananepho [A]366[A] "to return to soberness," as from a state of delirium or drunkenness said of those who, opposing the truth through accepting perversions of it, fall into the snare of the Devil, becoming intoxicated with error:

This "error" includes believing Satan's Lie about who and what we & others are in God, and his lie about the faithfulness and effectiveness of God's forgiveness and cleansing in our lives.

This "recovery" is possible only by "repentance unto the knowledge of the truth."

But, what TRUTH?
1. The truth about God.
2. The truth about yourself.
3. The truth about others.

Think of your shame and your bitterness as a ball and chain around your ankle. Everywhere you go, no matter who you are, or how important you are, you have to pick up that shame and bitterness and take it with you.

The lies that you believe are satan's lock that binds that ball and chain of shame and bitterness to you. When you break that lie, satan loses his hold and then you can say, *"I rebuke you satan, in Jesus' name. Get out!"* and he has to go!

D. The Source of this Recovery is a "Sound Mind."

1 Peter 5:8; *Be sober, be vigilant- because your adversary the devil, as a roaring lion, walketh about, seeking, whom he may devour:*

SOBER = nepho (nay'-fo); "to be free from the influence of intoxicants"...

"Soberness" that is a product of **"right thoughts"** or correct or factual thinking: thinking that is done with a clear or "sober" mind

If we are to be free from Satan's influence, we must be freed from the intoxicating delusion of his lies about God, others & ourselves.

Believing the truth about God's love for us, and the confirmation of the Holy Ghost bearing witness to our hearts, will bring us to the point of deliverance.

TOOL #3: Receiving The Miracle

What is the miracle? It is the manifested love of God.
(His love is manifested through presence, glory, power, fruits of the Spirit, works of the Spirit, and even blessings)

    A. This is done by Faith.

FAITH is the work! RECEIVING BY FAITH is the hardest work you will ever do.
This work is RELATIONAL. This is accepting, claiming, verbalizing, etc. As opposed to Believing which is a mental decision.

Take your miracle.

    Matthew 11:12; *And from the days of John the Baptist until now the kingdom of heaven suffereth violence, and the violent take it by force.*

Press your way in prayer and worship into your miracle.

    1 Titus 4:7 Exercise yourself unto Godliness.

    Ephesians 4:22-24; 22 That ye put off concerning the former conversation the old man, which is corrupt according to the deceitful lusts; **23 And be renewed in the spirit of your mind-, 24** And that ye **put on the new man**, which after God is created in righteousness and true holiness.

"Put on the New Man" is living out the miracle or making it real. As in Heaven, So on Earth.

We must discipline our hearts and minds to come daily into agreement with the truth.

TOOL #4: A Repentant Life

Seven times Paul called himself a "Prisoner of Jesus Christ."
Boundaries must be established and upheld if we are to retain the Glory in our lives.

Don't go back to a sinful lifestyle and expect to be able to live spiritual principles! A Repentant lifestyle is a must if we are to maintain victory over shame.

Forgiveness is how we get the healing!
Repentance helps to keep it! (Lifestyle of discipline)

TOOL #5: Pray for Others

When we have the routine of praying for others *(make a list of people in your life)*, we are able to identify any offenses we may have in our hearts.

Do an **inventory** on your heart.

TOOL #6: Prayer and Worship

      A. Obedience to the call to prayer! (Early Morning Prayer is an awesome intimate time with God.)

      B. Mentioning prayer is a casual reminding of God and remembering God and his blessings.

      C. Intercession for yourself and others is a deep passionate prayer, which brings breakthrough.

      D. Praying in the Holy Ghost! Praying in tongues is God praying for you through you. It is fellowship, and partnership (praying for others or situations that concern him or you where he and you are benefited.)

Grieving is not uncommon for people first moving towards this deep inner healing.

TOOL #7: Bible Reading

The most powerful tool in our arsenal is consistently reading the scriptures. We release all that Heaven has into our lives when we relate consistently with the Living Word.

Resources: The Bible Project on YouTube, Alpha's Bible in One Year, Bible Plans on the Bible App, RightNow Media, etc.

TOOL #8: Specific Declarations of Faith

The power of the spoken word and the power of agreement with God's word is a mighty tool in your arsenal.

Examples:
"God, I thank You that I am clean through Your Word."
"Lord, I receive Your great love for me."
"I thank You that I am crucified with Christ."
"I tread on the lion and the adder, the young lion and the dragon I trample under my feet!"
"Lord, I speak forgiveness to myself and to others."
"Lord, I ask You to forgive my enemy and have mercy upon him/her."

TOOL #9: OPTIONAL CHRISTLIKE FORGIVENESS?

Jesus teaches us to forgive, but on the cross, he exampled something far greater. He prayed for his enemies and asked God to forgive them. We are not instructed to do this, but the Bible says he is our example in all things.

If you wanna throw your healing into hyperdrive, don't just pray to forgive your enemy. Ask God to let them off the hook. Say, *"God you don't have to judge them for what they did to me. I'm asking for them as if they were asking for forgiveness. I want their record wiped clean."*

TOOL #10: LOVE EVERYBODY
Galatians 5:6; *"...but faith which worketh by love."*

John 13:34-35; *A new commandment I give unto you, That ye love one another; as I have loved you, that ye also love one another. 35 By this shall all men know that ye are my disciples, if ye have love one to another.*

John 15:9-13, 17; 9 *As the Father has loved me, so have I loved you. Abide in my love. 10 If you keep my commandments, you will abide in my love, just as I have kept my Father's commandments and abide in his love. 11 These things I have spoken to you, that my joy may be in you, and that your joy may be full. 12 "This is my commandment, that you love one another as I have loved you. 13 Greater love has no one than this, that someone lay down his life for his friends. You are my friends if you do what I command you…17 These things I command you, so that you will love one another.*

John 17:26; *I made known to them your name, and I will continue to make it known, that the love with which you have loved me may be in them, and I in them."*

1 Peter 1:22; *Now that you have purified yourselves by obeying the truth so that you have sincere love for each other, love one another deeply, from the heart.*

2 Timothy 1:7; *For God hath not given us the spirit of fear; but of power, and of love, and of a sound mind.*

2 Thessalonians 3:5; *And the Lord direct your hearts into the love of God, and into the patient waiting for Christ.*

1 Thessalonians 5:8; *But let us, who are of the day, be sober, putting on the breastplate of faith and love; and for an helmet, the hope of salvation.*

1 Thessalonians 4:9; *Now about your love for one another we do not need to write to you, for you yourselves have been taught by God to love each other.*

1 Thessalonians 3:12; *And the Lord make you to* **increase** *and* **abound in love** *one toward another, and toward ail men, even as we do toward you:*

Ephesians 3:16; 16 *that according to the riches of his glory he may grant you to be strengthened with power through his Spirit in your inner being,* **17** *so that Christ may dwell in your hearts through faith—that you, being rooted and grounded in love,* **18** *may have strength to comprehend with all the saints what is the breadth and length and height and depth,* **19 and to know the love of Christ** *that surpasses knowledge, that you may be filled with all the fullness of God.* **20** *Now to him who is able to do far more abundantly than all that we ask or think, according to the power at work within us,*

Love is the ANSWER!

REFLECTIONS & REVELATIONS

(Those things the Holy Spirit brings to mind)

Made in the USA
Middletown, DE
27 September 2024

61274689R00035